SACRED

RELATIONSHIPS:
LOVING FROM THE INSIDE OUT

by Rev. Danielle Hatchell, LCPC

Sacred Relationships: Loving From The Inside Out

Mail to:

Attn: Danielle Hatchell

9672 Marlboro Pike

Upper Marlboro, MD 20772

Website: http://daniellehatchell.com

Facebook: Expanding Growth Counseling and Wellness Center

Email: danielle@daniellehatchell.com

Bulk Ordering Information:

Special discounts are available on quantity purchases by corporations, associations and others. For details, contact the publisher at the address above.

Orders by U.S. trade bookstores and wholesalers contact the office of Expanding Growth at the contact information above.

A Special Note About How This Book Was Intentionally Created:

Dear Reader,

This book was initially created from a live interview. That's why it reads like a conversation rather than the traditional "book" that talks "at" you.

I wanted you to feel as though I'm talking "with" you much like a close friend or relative.

I felt that creating the book this way would make it easier for you to grasp the topics and put them to use quickly rather than wading through hundreds of pages.

So relax.

Grab a pen or pencil and some paper. Take notes and get ready to learn about how to create sacred relationships from the inside out.

Sincerely,

Rev. Danielle

Book Dedication

I dedicate this book to my daughters. May you grow to live and love fearlessly and know that you are worthy of your heart's desires.

May you be bold enough to endure the challenges in life and rise stronger than before, having learned your lessons well and used them to make new, empowered choices.

May God's love and grace be with you always and in all ways.

I love you both with my whole heart.

Mom ❤

Table of Contents

Chapter 1 -

My Journey

"She remembered who she was and the game changed." – Lalah Delia

I am a licensed professional counselor who has been in the field of counseling for over 20 years. I currently own and run a private practice in Maryland, and I absolutely love it. I feel incredibly honored to be trusted with my client's most vulnerable experiences and to be chosen to support them in healing and transforming their pain into power, regardless of the endless cases of trust related issues I see often in my line of duty. I always find deep satisfaction in seeing my clients overcome anxiety, depression, relationship difficulties and finding their way back home inside of themselves, sometimes for the first time in their lives. By home, I mean self-mastery. It is the time where we start to feel comfortable in our skin. We begin to feel love, value and appreciation for ourselves and our journey.

Professionally, I have a Bachelor's Degree in Psychology, a Master's Degree in Counselor Education and I am a Licensed Clinical Professional Counselor. However, it is by doing the healing work with my clients and in my own life that I have blossomed not only in my professional line of duty as a therapist but as a human being.

I believe that relationships are powerful learning opportunities for anyone who embraces the journey with an open heart. When we truly engage in relationships with our whole selves, body, mind, soul and spirit, we are in the process, using the opportunity to truly see who we are, the beauty that dwells within and also our pain. I specialize in supporting my clients with healing their relationships. This niche was a discovery through the struggles I experienced when I started to take romantic relationships seriously in my early 20s. At that time, I struggled to know who I was and also to know my self-worth and self-value because I didn't believe I was good enough. As a result, I attracted men who seemed to prove me right (the law of attraction taking its course).

I attracted men who cheated, lied and who even went as far as trying to change me to fit the image of who they thought I should be. Unfortunately, I conformed to make them happy and often lost myself in them. These were extremely painful experiences, especially when the relationships ended. I would feel broken. I was left to pick up the pieces and rediscover who I was time and time again.

So in an effort to transform these experiences, I had to take a deep look at myself. I did a personal assessment and then I realized that I was actually sourcing and creating all that was happening to me. I was the common denominator. I started to learn about manifestation and Universal Laws and Principals. I also began to understand my power. I worked on healing through coaching and Conscious Connected Breathing with amazing teachers, Ken and Renee Kizer. I changed my beliefs and built a healthier relationship with myself first, which transformed all of my relationships by doing my inner work. I thank God that I'm so much better now.

A large part of my healing also happened at the Inner Visions Institute for Spiritual Development. It's a school founded by Iyanla Vanzant. This was where I learned so much about healthy relationships, spirituality, prayer, meditation, effective communication, manifestation and so much more. Going through the process at Inner Visions supported me in healing my own relationships and growing into the woman I truly desired to be. My experiences at Inner Visions, gave me a great deal of the information that I have applied in the work I have done in my practice.

I established my private practice as a result of the work I did in the Personal Development Program of Inner Visions Institute for Spiritual Development and later, I completed the ministerial training through this program as well. In 2013, I was ordained as a Minister of Spiritual Consciousness, and today I am so blessed, I actually teach a relationships class and Conscious Connected Breathing class at Inner Visions. I am so grateful to be able to do the work that I love so much. I work with clients to develop healthier relationships in my private practice and I teach students about how to have healthy relationships as well.

So, it's like the old saying goes, "We teach what we need to learn." I didn't feel good enough and so I felt broken. What I later came to know and understand is that I was creating all of that relationship drama and pain. I was attracting partners who were willing participants to play a vital role in my drama and my healing. They got to be the villain and I had the opportunity to see myself and experience myself again as not good enough and broken. I was attracting the experiences I didn't want. When I finally realized that I was the source of it all, I began to see how powerful I really was. If I could unconsciously create painful experiences, then I could consciously create empowering and loving experiences. The moment I became clear about this, my life took a positive dimension.

When I learned to love myself and when I learned about manifestation, I began to recognize my worth, then I was able to transform and heal my relationships. It became a passion for me because I could see how I was able to transform my own experience. So I've really taken to teaching other people about knowing their worth, understanding who they are, understanding that they attract everything they experience and not just in relationships alone but literally everything in their lives. Today, I teach my clients how to create loving and fulfilling relationships by loving themselves first!

I have been married for almost 15 years. I met my husband in a Jow Ga Kung Fu martial arts school in Takoma Park, MD. At the time we first met, I was still on my learning curve in relationships and wasn't ready for the type of relationship he could offer. I was in the middle of doing the best I could with my work, as I was trying to understand healthy relationships, mostly by engaging in unhealthy ones. However, I was also learning more about who I was and who I wanted to be with, and I thank God for that. During that time, we had become friends, and we were friends for about four years before we actually started to date.

Today, he is unquestionably the love of my life. He is everything that I have ever prayed for, and I often tell him how grateful I am for him. It is a blessing to be in a relationship with someone who really understands me and accepts me for who I am, quirks and all. Today I realize that I had to accept all of me before I could be accepted by anyone else. He honors the parts of me that are wonderful and the parts that are not so wonderful, and I do the same for him.

Every day is another Divine opportunity for me to practice communicating and negotiating my desires because we don't always agree on everything. I get to practice allowing him to be who he is and accept him in all of his brilliance, and all of his faults as well. We are committed to each other and we're committed to growing our relationship and encouraging each other to be who we want to be, and to do the things in life that bring fulfillment to us both as individuals and as a couple.

I'm incredibly grateful to be on this journey of healing for lots of reasons. Not only because it has provided me the opportunity to create loving, joyful and authentic relationships but also because by diving deep in this work, I can now share it with you. I have met and married the love of my life. Together, we are blessed with two beautiful daughters and we are truly partners in every sense of the word. Our daughters are teenagers, so we have lots of opportunities to bond together, support, encourage and sometimes commiserate with one another.

Every day I get the opportunity to practice the things I teach my clients about having healthy boundaries, speaking their truth and asking for what they want in a relationship even when they're afraid of conflict or fear that their desires are inconvenient and especially when they're afraid of not being liked. I get the opportunity to get angry, act out and to forgive as well as ask to be forgiven. I also get the opportunity to love when it's easy and even when it's hard. I am so grateful and happy to have attracted a partner who is both willingly and open heartedly ready to do the work of relationship with me.

In this book, we will explore a concept which consists of three steps:

1. Evaluation

2. Identifying Beliefs

3. Visioning

This process will support you in beginning to create the type of sacred, loving relationships that you desire, by first understanding how to love yourself.

Every journey begins with a first step. And this book serves as a guide to creating loving, supportive and authentic relationships for everyone that takes all that is taught into step by step practice. Together we will discuss spiritual principles, concepts and tools that will support you in being successful and more productive in this very delicate, but vital area of your life. So this is where the work begins. I'm going to give you some specifics about what the work looks like, and how to move through it. Perhaps, you've been having a breakdown in relationships, or you've been stuck in a pattern of dysfunctional or dissatisfying relationships. Here's the first thing I will encourage you to do for you to start seeing yourself and your relationships differently.

Chapter 2 -

Fearless Moral Inventory

"Knowing yourself is the beginning of all wisdom."   *- Aristotle*

The first step in this process is **evaluation**. Imagine yourself to be a scientist, and you've been presented with a problem that needs to be solved. As a scientist, what you will first do is take the opportunity to evaluate and understand the problem. Scientists examine without judgment or scrutiny. They have a deep desire to create an outcome that they haven't seen before and they are committed to put in the work to make change happen. So with this book, you get the opportunity to become a scientist. The subject you are studying is you and the problem to be solved is how you engage in relationships.

I worked in the field of substance abuse for several years as an addiction's counselor. By doing this work, I learned about addiction and recovery. I developed a love and appreciation of the Twelve Steps of Recovery. I still today believe that we could all benefit from working through the steps. We each have problems in our lives that sometimes take over and create unnecessary pain. At times we even engage in addictive relationships. Step four in the twelve steps of Alcoholics Anonymous reads "(We) made a searching and fearless moral inventory of ourselves." When we do a fearless, moral inventory, we take the opportunity to examine and identify our challenges, and to be a demonstration of gentleness and courage so that these challenges can be healed.

To begin, you must evaluate and focus on understanding, and healing the relationship with yourself. Because the reality is that we attract, and we manifest our relationship experiences based on who we tell ourselves we are. So, if we have a broken relationship with ourselves, if we have an unfulfilled relationship with ourselves, if we're engaging in a lot of negative self-talk about who we are, if we diminish our worth and our value, then surely we will unconsciously attract those partners who will be a representation and reflection of those beliefs we hold about ourselves.

In this first step of your process, you get the opportunity to ask yourself questions like, "Who am I? What matters most to me? How do I demonstrate my worth and my value? Do I feel worthy enough to have what I want? How do I treat myself when things in my life are falling apart? Do I take time to celebrate my successes? Am I making major decisions in my life based on faith or fear? Am I satisfied with the way my life is unfolding? How would I describe my relationship with myself?"

The entire first step is about examining how you show up for yourself and how you relate to yourself. It's about becoming intimately acquainted with and accepting of those parts of you that you aren't comfortable posting on social media or allowing others to see. It is not about blaming, shaming or judging yourself (or anyone else!) It's about being honest, compassionate and authentic with yourself.

Too often, we focus too much attention to our relationships with other people, and the things that they do, (or don't do) or the way they make us feel. As a result of that, we don't focus on how we may be drawing those experiences to ourselves because of what we believe. So the first step is to find out who you are and assess where you are, in your relationship with yourself, and then you will start to do the work to heal any part of that relationship with yourself that seems to have gone out of alignment or is working against you and not for you.

There is no doubt, the work of changing your relationship with yourself will take time and consistent effort because research shows that it takes 21 days of focused attention to work on consistently changing a habit. I believe it takes this long for us to honestly assess the relationship with ourselves, and then start to work on it.

I encourage you to have fun with this process. Rebuilding or healing your relationship with yourself can be light hearted and joy filled as well. It doesn't have to be hard. Take yourself out on dates to places you enjoy spending time. If you aren't sure about what you like, experiment with different types of places and activities. Try placing reminders in the form of posted notes that say, "I love you," "I'm worthy," and "I matter." These notes will support you in creating a new internal dialog, a new way of speaking to yourself and thinking about yourself. It can be classified as a positive mental reshuffle. Take the time to write yourself love letters. If you notice that you engage in negative self talk, commit to changing the conversations you have with yourself by making them affirming and supportive. Learn to speak to yourself in the way you would speak to a close friend.

In order to change your relationship with yourself and take it to the level where you embrace and appreciate yourself every single day, you will have to commit to some type of practice that supports you in honoring yourself and loving yourself first.

Commit to doing this consistently for 21 days and see how you begin to shift. Notice how you speak to yourself and how you treat yourself after committing to doing this sacred work. **Yes, this is sacred work.** By learning to love, value and appreciate yourself, you are supporting yourself in being your best self and enjoying your life in the best way possible. Understanding that you are important and that you matter is sacred work, it's vital because it not only improves your life, it also touches the lives of those closest to you. As they watch you blossom, they also get inspired to grow and to heal as well.

Spirituality also plays a vital role in this process. In particular, the Law of Correspondence, also known as the Law of Attraction. The Law of Correspondence says that "like attracts like." We attract to us those experiences, people and the relationships that are a vibrational match. For example, if you're enjoying your relationship with yourself and you are genuinely feeling good about you, there is the tendency that you will attract people and situations that affirm that good feeling you have generated within yourself. On the other hand, if you're feeling unworthy or not good enough, then you literally attract or draw in energetically, that type of experience and those types of people that affirm such kind of experience as well.

When I learned about the Law of Attraction, I recognized that I was attracting the same type of person who reflected what I told myself was true about me, and that they were reflections of what I believed I was worthy of. I realized that because I felt poorly about myself, I was attracting experiences that proved those fears to be true. Not good enough was the negative core belief that I held about myself. So the energy and experiences that I was attracting affirmed that I wasn't good enough. I worked so hard to change my relationship with myself, so I could call in a better experience. It didn't take too long for an amazing shift to happen for me, and my relationships immediately changed as I finally understood that I held the key to creating the types of relationships I desired.

I finally realized that I was creating and manifesting relationships I didn't want to be in. I decided to change the way I was thinking about myself and to change the old, outdated ideas that I held about who I was, so I could start to attract the types of experiences that were a reflection of where I wanted to be, who I wanted to be, and what I wanted to experience.

That was the first step for me in healing my relationships, and also part of the big work I do with my clients. I support them in understanding that they are creating the relationships they have with others based on the relationship they have with themselves and that they have the power and the ability to improve their relationships by changing these thoughts and beliefs, which they hold about themselves. This first step is about learning how to love yourself fully, fiercely and unapologetically.

Chapter 3 -

Understanding the Power of Your Beliefs

"Beliefs have the power to create and the power to destroy." – Tony Robbins

The second step to creating sacred relationships is to **get clear about the beliefs you're holding about love and relationships.** What do you believe to be true about relationships for you? This is such an important step in the process because remember that we create experiences from the beliefs we hold. And so, it's important for you to be truly clear with that. So many times, when I'm working with clients, they say, "Oh well, I think that relationships are great" but in actuality, they are having a horrible time in their relationships.

In moments like this, where there is a clear disconnect, I encourage them to go deeper. I ask them to describe to me the experience they're having with love and relationships because this experience is actually a manifestation of their beliefs. If they have difficult experiences in relationships, what are some of the beliefs that are fueling those experiences? We then take the time to honestly assess the beliefs they hold about love, about relationships, about marriage and the partners they attract.

These beliefs often come from experiences we had growing up, such as watching the way adults around us behaved in their relationships. Watching my mother and father, I learned that relationships were hard and that commitment was the engine that kept a marriage running. They were married for 38 years. They met when they were 13 and 14 years old. They stayed together until my mom made her transition in 2013. They were together for a very long time; they were children when they first met. I watched them go through their ups and downs in their relationship. I understood that they loved each other but on their journey of growing and maturing, they weren't kind to each other.

At times it looked like they were doing hard prison time, together. Sometimes they were happy together but most of the time, they were not.

As I watched their relationship unfold over the years, my thought was, "Relationships suck. I don't want to do that!" Deep down, I believed that my relationships would look like my parents' relationship, and I most certainly did not want to do that. So it's interesting when I think about where my beliefs came from about relationships. I now see that I was starting to navigate them and not really wanting to be in them. I was afraid of opening my heart due to the fear of being hurt.

In most of my relationships that I attracted at that time, I felt like I was doing hard time, just like my parents. I didn't feel valued, I didn't feel seen, I didn't feel loved, and I got hurt. These were the types of relationships I didn't want. Since I believed I would be hurt in relationships, I attracted hurtful experiences time and time again until the pain became so intense that I finally woke up and decided to create a new experience.

It's by understanding those beliefs that you hold about the person that you're attracted to and the experience that you're going to have, that you can see the type of relationship experiences you've been attracting to you.

If you can see those beliefs, identify them and understand them, you have the power to change those beliefs. When you change your beliefs, you can start to attract the types of relationships that you consciously create from your desires, not your fears. The types of relationships that feel good, build you up, and bring joy and passion.

Most people have a tendency to think about the type of person they would like to attract, but they think very little about the type of relationship experience they'd like to have with them. How does a person start to create in their mind the experience that they actually want because the other person on the other hand has some say too? So how do you do that?

This is where we get to see if the person that we have attracted is a vibrational match because truly it's a matter of agreement. So what's the agreement in terms of the experience that you both desire to have in the relationship together? And if the desires you both hold do not align, if you both don't choose to have an experience that is complementary of the other, chances are the relationship is probably not going to last.

It is unloving for us to force our partner to be in a relationship with us that fulfills our desires but in turn disregards their needs and desires. In the same way our partners can't force us to be in a relationship with them and in the way that they want it, if it disregards our needs and desires.

Loving relationships are about coming together and agreeing on the type of relationship we want to experience together. It's about compromise and finding the win, win. Love and mutual respect are key ingredients to a successful and sacred relationship. Loving relationships thrive where there is trust. We need to feel free to be who we are at our core and feel valued and appreciated.

So many times in the past, I have felt like I had to be someone else so that my partner could be happy. I tried to be who I thought they wanted me to be. But as I grew, I understood that every time I engaged in those types of relationships, I lost myself and I was miserable. It was a form of self-betrayal. So my approach to healing included saying, "No More!" to those types of relationships. The experience I chose to create consciously was to give myself full permission to be who I am and only engage myself with partners who were willing to do the same. It's about having clear conversations about our desires and cleanly communicating through disagreements.

Sacred relationships are built on having clear and realistic boundaries. We create these healthy boundaries by talking openly with our partners about who we are and what we want as well as our rules of engagement in relationships, such as what works for us and what doesn't. Through clear, authentic communication, we can see if this relationship will be a match for us or not, based on how our boundaries are honored.

This is why Step One is so important. By understanding who we are and finding love and appreciation for ourselves, we will be able to create healthy boundaries and communicate them clearly to a potential partner so there can be an agreement. It is critical to have conversations about the experience we want to create in our relationships with our partners, that will help clarify what we each want in a relationship, and to see if those desires are a match. There may even be room for compromise, but it's important that these compromises are healthy for you and your partner.

So, let's say you've been doing your work to understand the beliefs you hold about a relationship and you are getting clear about the experience you'd like to have in the relationship, and you get stuck. What do you do? What if you're having a hard time honestly identifying what you believe? The key is to go back to the common themes that have been showing up for you in your relationships.

What is it that you're experiencing? What has been showing up for you, what have you actually been manifesting? Are you attracting people who are dishonest, non-committal or critical? If you are, then the belief is that men or women are dishonest, non-committal or critical. Those are the beliefs that are manifesting those experiences. If you find out that you attract partners who don't value and appreciate you for being who you are, and at the end of those relationships, you are left feeling that you don't have permission to be yourself. Then the belief is, "I can't be myself and be loved." Another thing we tell ourselves in these experiences is that "I'm just too _____ in a relationship." You can fill in the blank with words like needy, loving, independent, vulnerable, honest, open, etc.

Any relationship that leaves you feeling that it's not okay to be who you are and grow into being your best self, is not one you're meant to be in. Any relationship that requires you to be perfect to be worthy of love, is unrealistic and unhealthy. Healthy relationships are created by couples who agree on the experiences they'd like to create in the relationship and by people who give each other permission to be exactly who they are, without feeling the need to fix, change or control the other person.

Once you are complete with this step, I encourage you to start writing out new beliefs that will support you in consciously creating the relationships you desire. It would also be helpful to write out the qualities of the person you would like to attract. Examples of more supportive beliefs are, "I believe that I can create, loving relationships, I believe that I am worthy of being loved for being who I am, or I believe that it is safe for me to be my most vulnerable, authentic self in relationships."

Examples of a list of the types of partners you would like to attract may look like this: "I attract partners who are honest, adventurous, accepting, passionate, genuine, integrous, loving, kind, humorous, etc."

If you get stuck on understanding what the beliefs are, then you get the Divine opportunity to start paying closer attention to the relationship experiences you have been manifesting, and understand what the belief is underneath the manifestations. And it really just takes the time to pause and to get clear about your beliefs. I encourage you to take time out to write in a journal, and simply allow yourself to be truly honest. Remember the Fearless Moral Inventory. It's where you allow yourself to be straightforward about what you're actually experiencing, not just what you want to experience. In essence, you can't heal what you won't acknowledge. When you can identify and acknowledge the truth about what isn't working in your relationships, you'll be able to heal and consciously create the relationship you desire.

Chapter 4 -

Clarifying Your Vision

"Vision is the first step toward building the future we desire, the life through which we can experience fulfillment and a sense of accomplishment. Vision gives us hope, direction and a path to follow." - Alan Seale

The third step in this process of creating sacred relationships is to become aware of what you truly desire. In this step you will explore the concept by asking yourself the following question, "What is the highest vision that I hold for my love relationships?" This vision that you hold for your love relationships is not about the fairy tales that you've read as a child. Your vision is not about what you learned about relationships just by reading romance novels, watching TV or seeing a romantic comedy at the movies. That's someone else's romanticized notion of what a relationship could be. In this third step, you get the opportunity to become clear about what it is that you envision for yourself in a relationship so that you will be able to manifest it.

This process is called **visioning**. Visioning is the development of a goal or a clear idea that leads to the implementation of that goal in the future. Visioning is about figuring out what you want your successful outcome to look like. In relationship visioning, you are figuring out what your successful relationship will look like. You will then allow yourself to hold this vision of this relationship in your heart and your mind's eye. You can see the image of this success; you can feel the excitement of a dream come true.

Visions are powerful because they propel us forward. And this vision has to be enticing and compelling enough to lure us into action. As we pursue our vision, we are urged to grow and challenge those aspects of ourselves that may even be frightened by the call to go higher, to risk disappointment, to fall and be courageous enough to rise again. Relationships involve risk, and there are no guarantees. So I ask you, is the highest vision you hold about your relationships compelling enough for you to take that risk? If not, you now have a Divine opportunity to create such a vision and to allow that vision to boldly pull you forward.

There are many ways to use visioning. A few of which are most used are guided imagery and vision boards,

- Guided imagery is a form of meditation that will allow you to see and experience your goal in your mind's eye. This is a powerful way to envision your desired experience. Through meditation, you have the opportunity to clarify the relationship experience that your heart desires. This technique will allow you to feel the love and imagine the acceptance you long for in your relationships.

- Vision boards clarify the highest and best vision you hold in your heart for your sacred relationships as you call them forth into manifestation.

You can create a vision board by finding images, words, and phrases that elicit an emotional response that is in alignment with the type of relationship you desire to experience. You can create vision boards on an app on your phone or do it the hands-on way by cutting images and words out of magazines. When you complete your vision board, place it in an environment where you can see the creation and remember what you are going for. This will create a mighty energetic space for your desires to manifest. When you become clear about the relationship you want, it will become almost impossible for you to settle for less than that. This is the power of your vision at work.

This step is about allowing yourself to see, experience and feel the type of relationship you desire to have within yourself and with a significant other. This is the part of the law of attraction that people often might miss. By doing this, you become a vibrational match for the relationships you want to have. You create this by aligning your feelings with the experience you envision. For example, if you are seeking to create loving relationships in your life, allow yourself to feel that love in your life now. Allow yourself to feel as if you have already manifested the relationship you want, as if it is happening right now.

You are so much more powerful than you know. You are really in the driver's seat of your life. You are made in the image and likeness of God and are endowed with the gift of creation.

You create with your thoughts. Your thoughts are powerful. The way that you think about your life, yourself, your experiences, and the beliefs that you hold are extremely powerful and out picture as the experiences you create in your life.

Most people don't realize that they've been creating unconsciously with that power. The shift happens when you allow yourself to know that you're powerful and deserving of the experiences and relationships that you truly want to have within yourself and with a significant other. When you allow yourself to shift your energy into consciously creating the experience that you desire to have, that's when the magic happens. That's when you start to attract new affirming partners and relationships or at the very least, when you are able to say no to the types of relationships that no longer serve you.

Through the use of visioning, you will start to see that your thoughts are powerful, and when your thoughts and your feelings are aligned with the experience that you truly desire to have, the likelihood of you manifesting that which you envision is truly great. Not only do you have the power to create the relationships you desire, but you are the power!

Again, I encourage you to have fun with this process! Throw a vision board party, have others join the fun and get excited about the experiences they want to manifest in their lives too. Especially, if this work starts to feel too heavy or challenging for you. Vision board parties are popular because they are enjoyable. They create a space for you to consciously create the experience you want in the spirit of joy and celebration with people you love. Now, *that* creates a powerful vibration! Imagine the experiences you will manifest with that type of energy.

This step is about creating and living your vision for love on a daily basis. You are consciously creating this area of your life and deciding what it will be for you. You do this by unplugging from the limiting thoughts that tell you that you aren't worthy of the right kind of love or partner for you or that they don't exist. You permit yourself to move your love life, with intention, in the direction you would like it to go. You also permit yourself to allow it to happen. It is, as well, about being very deliberate because you've spent some time with your vision, you've allowed yourself to get clear about who you are, what you believe and what you truly desire, and you're actively moving your life in that direction.

Chapter 5 -

Getting Unstuck

"The only way to get what you really want is to let go of what you don't want." – Iyanla Vanzant

At times I have seen my clients wasting time, by not going in the direction that they truly desire to go. They're on a path, and it's not that it's a wrong path but it's a path that's not aligned with what they truly desire. They have been committed to unproductive cycles and patterns of behavior, such as settling for partners who are incapable of meeting their relationship needs. Although, these behaviors may have even worked at some point in their lives, now they contribute to them not just being stuck alone but also attracting the types of relationships they want nothing to do with. I call this getting lost in the weeds.

As they start to do the work of healing their relationships, they start to recognize the unhealthy and unconscious beliefs that have supported them in manifesting unhealthy relationships, and then they start to beat themselves up. This is when they get lost in the weeds. Then they say to themselves, "Why didn't I know this sooner? Why couldn't I've known this in my last relationship?" "I could have saved myself so much heartache and pain, or I could have even had a family by now."

They start to beat themselves up for having the difficult relationships they have had because they didn't know then what they know now. So it's a place where people get stuck and where they waste energy and time. I see it happen often. When I do, I remind them that their spiritual journey is exactly what it's supposed to be. We learn from all of our experiences and they unfold at the time and space they are supposed to happen. Our healing occurs in it's own Divine timing.

The time that we spent learning what we've learned, and having those experiences that didn't feel great, is quite valuable. So it's imperative that we understand that there are no mistakes in this process, and it is all unfolding the way that it's supposed to unfold. The biggest lessons in this process, are to first, learn how to grant yourself grace and second to find gratitude for the journey, regardless of how challenging it has been so far.

My book coach Sensei Subira Folami, had a wonderful way of summing up this concept. She shared her beautiful wisdom with me when she said, "I find it helpful to remind myself that nature doesn't waste anything. If you look at it how nature works, it recycles, it reuses, it transforms, it transmutes, but there's no trash can for nature. It decomposes and becomes something else. Your experience is not wasted, instead it is serving to transform you into who you were created to be."

Another challenge that I see people face is having an unrealistic and romanticized perception of how relationships are supposed to look. Such perception blinds them from appreciating the person who stands before them. An example of an unrealistic concept is when you are expecting your lover to know your every thought, feeling and desire without you having to say it. We make them responsible for tending to our uncommunicated desires and punish them when they don't get it right. The reality is, nobody's going to read your mind. If you have a desire, it's your responsibility to articulate it and bring that desire to your lover's awareness.

A different type of stuck point happens when you start to believe that you can't have what you want because you keep experiencing difficult relationships over and over again.

When you've been manifesting the same experience, you can start to engage in distorted ways of thinking and believe that these thoughts are true.

These thought patterns are called *cognitive distortions*. They are defined as *exaggerated or irrational thought patterns that cause us to have a false sense of reality.* One of the most common cognitive distortions is called *overgeneralization*.

When we are engaging the thought pattern off overgeneralization, we see certain aspects operating in our lives as a never-ending pattern of defeat. We expect to be unsuccessful. What do you think happens when you expect to have unsuccessful relationships? You will definitely attract unsuccessful relationships. You are no longer a vibrational match for the healthy relationship that you want because you expect the opposite of that experience. The truth is that you are having a more difficult time attracting the relationship you desire because you don't think it could happen for you. I encourage you to push past these limiting beliefs.

When you have a clear intention and believe that you are worthy of change, change happens. If you find yourself entertaining relationships that aren't good for you, you have the power to say no and to make a new choice.

Focus on the good you desire to create in your life and get excited about the change you are creating. Use past relationships as stepping stones on your healing journey and take the time to learn the necessary lessons they are here to teach you.

So, let's say that you've got affirming notes posted around your house, and you've been having affirming conversations with yourself, and it could as well be that you've been taking yourself out on dates. Let's say you've been feeling good about yourself and your life and then that phone call comes in or a conversation happens which leads to an argument or disagreement. It could be a call from your mother, your father, or an ex-partner. That phone call happens, and all of a sudden you get stuck back into the negative self-talk and hurt feelings you started with after you have done so much work to change and what's worse is that you can't seem to get unstuck. What can you do?

It's easy for you to get stuck because you've been engaging these patterns of behaviors and getting triggered by some key people or certain types of people for years, probably even decades. Some of these responses of anger or self-defense may be rooted in how you survived difficult times as a child. This is your journey and you are doing it on your own. In this case, journaling is extremely supportive because it helps you to identify what you are feeling and can really give you some insight into changes that you can make to improve your situation. But let's say that you've been diligently using your journal, and you get the phone call or see the text message or social media post, and you still go through the roof, forget all the work that you've been putting in and can't seem to break through. The thing to do at this time is to hire a counselor or coach.

When we are doing our inner work, we sometimes get to the point in our journey where we've taken ourselves as far as we can go. Eliciting the support of a relationship coach, or even a counselor to support you in working through some of those more deep-seated issues would be beneficial. A coach or a counselor can support you in discovering the breakthrough in healing your relationship with yourself. Much of the work that I do in my counseling practice is with women who want to improve their relationships. Through therapy, they begin to intimately understand the relationship they have with themselves and discover how they developed this type of relationship. I then further support them in understanding how to make their relationships with themselves better and to do the work to have the type of relationship with themselves, which they would like to see mirrored outside of themselves. I teach them how to treat themselves the way they would like to be treated by others. It is definitely an inside job and once you change the inner experience, you can as well change the outer experiences.

Chapter 6 -

Great Opportunities Await You

"Opportunity is missed by most people because it is dressed in overalls and looks like hard work."   *– Thomas Edison*

Whether you are a novice in relationships or quite experienced, there are amazing opportunities available for you by committing to do this work. It begins when you learn how to be in a loving relationship with yourself and how to love and truly appreciate your life.

I tell people all the time, it's when we get into that space of gratitude, when we are just living our lives and having a good time and not worried about relationships or anything else, we actually up the level our energy.

When I talk about being a vibrational match, it is about aligning your energy to the experience you desire. You can't create a peaceful existence by constantly being at war with yourself and others. You can create a peaceful life by deciding to align with the energy of peace and committing to think and act in a peaceful manner no matter what life brings your way. This is how to align your energy to the experience you desire to create for yourself.

The same is true for your relationships. You can't attract the type of relationship you desire by expecting to have unsuccessful relationships or staying committed to being in and maintaining relationships that are painful and disappointing. Decide to be in relationships that feel good to you and which mirror the experience you desire. You will be able to make space for these relationships when you stop engaging in relationships that feed your fears, pain and insecurities. I encourage you to find joy in living and loving your life. Then you will attract all types of wonderful experiences.

Great opportunities await you! The greatest opportunity is in learning how to fall in love with yourself and the life you have created for yourself.

If there's a part of your life, that isn't really working for you, you get the opportunity to do the work to heal and transform it.

By doing so, you will learn to appreciate that part of your life as well. So, learning how to embrace self is the biggest opportunity in all of this. And as you do that, you obtain the key to unlock the experiences and relationships in your life that you truly desire.

Chapter 7 -

Managing Your Time

"My favorite things in life don't cost any money. It's really clear that the most precious resource we all have is time." – Steve Jobs

It would be supportive to allow this inner work to inspire you. I encourage you to break this work up into small increments and to develop mechanisms to manage your time. Here are some helpful ways:

- Set reminders on your phone to schedule thirty minutes to one hour of uninterrupted time a day to do this work.

- Journal insights about your current relationship with yourself and about the type of love you want to grow within yourself.

- The next day, commit to a window of time to search for images that will support you in feeling excited and clarifying the experience that you would like to have in your relationships.

- Perhaps another day, you would choose to spend your time getting clear by writing in your journal about feelings that come up for you when you think about your past relationships and lessons learned.

Think of this as artistic time because you are consciously creating something wonderful, while you're journaling, and clarifying your new beliefs or creating a vision board.

This is an opportunity to create powerful and life-altering change. This creative time allows you to be clear about the direction you want your life to grow into. Allow yourself to be excited by it!

What does becoming the love of your life feel like and what is the greatest adventure you can envision for this sacred love? Does this new vision of love inspire you? Does it give you hope? If it does, then you are definitely on the right path and if it doesn't, it's okay to go back to the drawing board and try again.

Chapter 8 -

The Tools of Reality Creation

"You were born with potential. You were born with goodness and trust. You were born with ideals and dreams. You were born with greatness. You were born with wings. You are not meant for crawling, so don't. You have wings. Learn to use them and fly!" - Rumi

You are creating a new reality of sacred relationships. And in doing that, some tools can support you in your process of creation. They are called the **tools of reality creation**. When I first learned about this process, I was a student at Inner Visions and I was mesmerized. We were introduced to this concept through a book by Lazaris entitled The Sacred Journey: You And Your Higher Self. My ego mind had a hard time believing that it could be easy, but because I have used these tools throughout the years, I have found that it doesn't have to be hard, and these tools do really work when we use them to our benefit. You can use these tools to shift your experience and begin to create consciously. The essential tools for reality creation are desire, imagination and expectancy.

Let's start by looking at how the first tool, *desire*, plays a part in creating our reality. When we resonate with desire, we tap into our heart center. We are able to manifest with our desires because we have a longing for the experience that we're going for, we crave it. When the word desire is broken down, it literally means de-sire or of God. When we hold a strong desire, we wield great power. So it's about allowing yourself to hold a strong desire for the experience that you are seeking to manifest. In this case, it is about having a strong desire for the type of love you seek to create within yourself and with others.

The second tool of reality creation is *imagination*. When you start to work with imagination, you are engaging the law of attraction. You are giving yourself the permission to envision the beautiful experience of love that you desire to create in your life. Give yourself permission to close your eyes, visualize it, and feel the emotions that wash over you as you experience this love. Imagine that you're walking in and living the type of love, type of life, and the type of relationship that you desire. Where will you be going? What is the trip going to look like? What is it like getting up and making breakfast in the morning with your love? Just permit yourself to see it in real time as if it is happening now.

The third tool of reality creation is *expectancy*. This is the place where most people are challenged because they are seeking to manifest the desire of their heart but they don't expect those desires to happen for them. They can even imagine a sacred love, but the expectancy is what's lacking. Expectancy is a key ingredient to reality creation. The tool of expectancy is about you believing that you can and will attract sacred love relationships. It is about believing that this experience of great love will happen in your life, not just in the lives of others. And so, for most of us, it's really about up-leveling our expectancy, and our belief that whatever it is that we desire can actually come to us, and happen for us.

Chapter 9 -

A Success Story

"We delight in the beauty of the butterfly, but rarely admit the changes it has gone through to achieve that beauty." – Maya Angelou

As a therapist, sometimes I do long-term therapy. There is a young woman I've worked with for several years who completely transformed her life by healing her relationship with herself. When she came to me, she was in a long term relationship. She had serious challenges in the relationship. She didn't feel seen, supported, loved or valued. Her work experiences were also challenging and unfulfilling. She had been committed to her relationship and her job for so long that she believed she was supposed to stay and see things through. Eventually she married her boyfriend. For a while, a part of her was convinced that the relationship and her job defined her and gave her a sense of purpose.

She did her work in counseling to understand who she was, and to help her see her value and her worth and to start appreciating herself for being who she was, her unique gifts and even her flaws. Essentially, her whole self. When she started to do her inner work, in an effort to heal her relationship with herself, she was able to shift her outer experiences. This new experience of self love and self-appreciation also extended itself into her relationships.

She began to clearly see that she was having the same experience at work that she was having in her marriage. At work she also didn't feel valued, seen, accepted or respected. She understood eventually that she was creating this experience. So she delved deeper into her inner work, and became even more determined to heal. In doing this, she became crystal clear about who she was and the experience she wanted to have in all of her relationships. Then she was able to start to shift the interactions with people on the outside, even at work.

Eventually, her marriage dissolved because as she grew in her love for herself, this relationship was no longer a vibrational match. She expected to be treated with love and respect and was no longer willing to be treated as though she did not matter. She could no longer be with a person who was not meeting her where she was or who was unwilling to grow with her.

She up-leveled who she was and the experience that she desired to have within herself in a relationship. The release of this relationship opened avenues for new and exciting love experiences.

She eventually found new employment in a job where she was valued, treated with respect, able to excel, grow and be promoted. As she up-leveled, by expecting to be treated with respect, she became a vibrational match for the work relationships she truly desired to experience in her life.

Currently, she is clear about who she is and what she wants and she operates her life in integrity. She is no longer comfortable entertaining people who reflect her old beliefs about not being enough. She's attracting experiences within romantic relationships that feel better to her where she has a voice, where she feels confident communicating what she wants and what she doesn't want.

Today she has powerful boundaries that govern all of her relationships and she isn't afraid to communicate those boundaries. She's having more fun in her life than ever before. She is going on more frequent vacations, traveling and experiencing the world. As she has released her old relationship baggage, she is also physically releasing weight from her body. She's feeling good in her skin and she is learning to love herself, and live the type of life she has always wanted.

In her life experience, she's now actually able to see how she creates her experiences, and she seeks to consciously create what she wants. Today she believes that she is worthy. None of that could have happened until she was able to learn how to love and accept herself and believe that she was worthy of living the type of life that her heart desired.

Chapter 10 -

The Bottom Line -
You Are Worthy

*For I know the plans I have for you," declares
the Lord, "plans to prosper you and not to harm
you, plans to give you hope and a future.*

Jeremiah 29:11 NIV

You are 100% worthy of the type of life and love that you dream about for yourself. It all starts within. If you can create a sacred, more loving, affirming and satisfying relationship with yourself, then you can create those same loving, affirming, and satisfying relationships with others. The key to changing your relationships is in your hand. Your love is the love you've been waiting for. It is that love that has the power to change your life and to start you on the path to anything your heart desires. When you stop looking for that love to come through someone else and you are able to find that love within, surely magic will happen.

God, life, and the Universe are fully ready to support your desires and intentions for the sacred relationships you seek to create in your life.

Use this process with an open mind and an open heart. Allow yourself to be supported by the prayers and intentions you create as you move through this process, and invite your close friends to join you in your quest. Whether you have met the love of your life in partnership or are still seeking, this process can support you.

This process of:

1. evaluating and healing your relationship with yourself

2. up leveling the beliefs you hold about relationships and

3. envisioning of the type of relationship you truly desire, will support you in strengthening all of your relationships.

When you do the work to heal your relationship with yourself, all of your relationships will be transformed. That is the power of healing and love in action! I believe in you and I send my prayers and positive intentions to join you as you work through this process.

Be bold!

Be loved!

Be blessed!

Rev. Danielle

Made in the
USA
Middletown, DE